Joke Busters

SUPERHERO STARS

JOHN BYRNE

■SCHOLASTIC

**For Susila and Richard –
real superheroes!**

Scholastic Children's Books,
Commonwealth House, 1-19 New Oxford Street,
London WC1A 1NU, UK
A division of Scholastic Ltd
London ~ New York ~ Toronto ~ Sydney ~ Auckland
Mexico City ~ New Delhi ~ Hong Kong

Published in the UK by Scholastic Ltd, 2003

Text and illustrations copyright © John Byrne, 2003

ISBN 0 439 97738 X

All rights reserved
Printed by Nørhaven Paperback A/S, Denmark

2 4 6 8 10 9 7 5 3 1

The right of John Byrne to be identified as the author and illustrator
of this work has been asserted by him in accordance with
the Copyright, Designs and Patents Act, 1988.

YOU'RE JUST IN TIME, JOKE BUSTERS! I'M AGENT GIGGLE AND THIS IS MY PARTNER AGENT GROAN. ONCE AGAIN WE'RE ON A MISSION TO COLLECT THE WORLD'S BEST JOKES!

YES, AND SINCE ALL THESE JOKES ARE ABOUT SUPERHEROES AND SUPERVILLAINS IT'S GOING TO BE A SUPER-DIFFICULT TASK!

Could you help us out? But first you'll need to pass the...

OFFICIAL
Joke Busters
SECURITY CHECK!

OFFICIAL
Joke Busters
SECURITY CHECK!

1 Do you have incredible super strength?
a) Yes
b) No
c) Sorry, I can't answer the question ... the pen is too heavy for me to lift.

2 Do you wear a cool costume?
a) Yes
b) No
c) You'll have to repeat that question ... my mask keeps falling down over my eyes.

3 Do you believe in Truth and Justice?
a) Yes
b) No
c) Of course I do ... Well, actually,
   I copied this answer from the
   person sitting beside me.

HOW DID YOU DO?

THERE ARE NO RIGHT ANSWERS! BUT WHETHER YOU ARE A JOKE-BUSTING EXPERT OR JUST A BEGINNER BUSTER, YOUR JOKE COLLECTION'S ABOUT TO BE

SUPERCHARGED

BY THE FOLLOWING PAGES!

SO WHAT ARE WE WAITING FOR? UP, UP AND AWAY!

THE BATBLOKE AND ROBERT JOKE FILE

THESE GUYS SAY THEY'RE THE TOP CRIME-FIGHTING DUO AROUND. I THOUGHT WE WERE THE TOP CRIME-FIGHTING DUO AROUND! AGENT GIGGLE

WHY DOES BATBLOKE NEED A PARTNER?

BECAUSE WHEN HE'S ON HIS OWN HE GETS IN A FLAP!

7

8

9

LOOK, SUPERHERO-ING IS TOUGH THESE DAYS. WE'VE HAD TO CUT DOWN A LITTLE. NOW STOP MOANING AND YOU CAN JOIN ROBERT AND ME AT THE BUS STOP!

IS YOUR NEIGHBOUR A SUPERHERO?

OF ALL A SUPERHERO'S POWERS, PERHAPS THE MOST AMAZING IS THE ABILITY TO HIDE THEIR REAL IDENTITY FROM FRIENDS AND NEIGHBOURS...

... AT LEAST THEY HIDE IT UNTIL WE RUIN IT FOR THEM BY GIVING YOU THESE SUPER-SPOTTING TIPS!

TIP 1

Does lots of mail get delivered to your neighbour's house with a different name on it? This could mean your neighbour is a superhero ... or that your postman's not super-good at his job.

ELECTROMAN
2 ORDINARY RD
NORMALVILLE

TIP 2

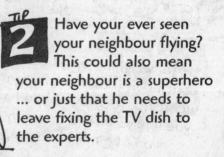

Have your ever seen your neighbour flying? This could also mean your neighbour is a superhero ... or just that he needs to leave fixing the TV dish to the experts.

12

TIP 3 Have you seen your neighbour in an amazing car?

ZOOOOM!

This could certainly mean your neighbour is a superhero ... or simply that your neighbour found a way around the trick on page 10 of the book!

TIP 4 If your neighbour's house is regularly attacked by giant robots, there is a very good chance that your neighbour is a superhero.

GRR!

OH NO! MY LAWN!

After weighing up all the evidence, our conclusion is that your neighbour is not a superhero. (Because if you have any sense, you'll have moved house by now so you won't be neighbours any more!)

NUMBER 1 TUFF TEACHER!

What is its super power?
The power to keep you after school as late as possible.

What is its secret identity?
Very cleverly disguises the fact that he is a teacher by not actually knowing anything.

Where is its secret hideout?
Hides behind bike sheds, looking for reasons to keep you late after school.

What is its weakness?
Food. (Must be why he confiscates all your goodies.)

Name: The Pun-Guin

Crimes Committed: Most people say every joke that comes out of my mouth is a crime.

Have you been in prison? Never for long. I just start telling my jokes and the wardens help me to escape.

Is there any superhero you're scared of? Snakeman.

Because snakes are scary? No. Because snakes have no ears ... they can't hear my jokes.

16

17

SPECIAL NIGHT EDITION FOR SUPERHEROES WHO HAVE ORDINARY JOBS DURING THE DAY!

SUPER SIGNAL SLIP UP!

One of the city's most famous superheroes has had to change his name to "Flatbloke" after his searchlight signal accidentally dazzled one of his flying friends who fell on top of him.

Serves him right for leaving the landing light on.

THIS IS EXACTLY THE KIND OF DISASTER THAT DRIVES YOU BATS!

20

WHERE DID SOUPERMAN SLEEP ON THE SCHOOL TRIP?

IN HIS CLARK TENT!

WHO GETS THE LOWEST MARKS AT SUPERHERO SCHOOL?

THE X-MEN

WHY WASN'T THE SUPERTEACHER PLEASED WHEN THE HUNK BROUGHT HIM AN APPLE?

OOPS!

BECAUSE HE FORGOT TO TAKE IT OFF THE TREE FIRST!

SUPERHERO SCHOOL ORCHARD KEEP OUT

Joke Busters
Guide to
REAL VILLAINS

NUMBER 2 SUPERMUM!

What is its super power?
Can affect the future – every time she says,
"Wear your coat, it will rain!" and you don't,
it does.

What is its secret identity?
May be a clone – everyone we know has a mum
like this!

Where is its secret hideout?
Doesn't need one – she storms into your room
without knocking. And there's no point you
having a hideout 'cos supermum has eyes in the
back of her head!

Name: Wanda Woman

Superpowers: Able to fly, grant wishes and send people to the ball.

Hang on ... that sounds like the fairy godmother? Ssh! I'm trying to update my image.

How have you done that? Well, I've got myself a really flash "Wandamobile".

Can we see it? Er... No. Unfortunately it's just turned back into a pumpkin.

Your superhero hero: Osbert Sparkleton

Who's that? My nephew. He's promised to lend me his comic collection so I can learn the names of real superheroes.

27

URGENT
MESSAGE
FOR ALL CUSTOMERS OF

HUNT THE HERO!

OK, JOKE BUSTERS—
IT'S TIME TO TEST
YOUR BUSTING
BRAIN POWER!
ON THE NEXT PAGE
IS A GROUP OF
ORDINARY PEOPLE
AND ONE SUPERHERO
USING HIS AMAZING
POWERS OF DISGUISE!
CAN <u>YOU</u> SPOT
THE SUPERHERO?

30

DID **YOU** SPOT THE {**SUPERHERO**}?

If you couldn't spot the superhero on this page, don't worry ... because the superhero we mean is the amazing transparentman. Funny, though ... we were certain you'd see right through him.

BATBLOKE'S

WHAT DO BATS SING WHEN IT'S WET?

RAINDROPS KEEP FALLING ON MY FEET!

WHAT SHOULD YOU DO TO A TIRED BAT?

RECHARGE HIS BAT-TERY!

WHAT DO BATS USE TO BREAK DOWN DOORS?

A BAT-TERING RAM!

FAVOURITE BAT JOKES!

THE INCREDIBLE HUNK

JOKE FILE

Some heroes turn green and monstrous when they're angry. This one is green, not modest and makes everybody else angry! AGENT GROAN

WHAT DID THE HUNK THINK OF HIS NEW SHIRT?

RIPPING! —

RIPPLE!

FLEX!

BULGE!

WHAT DO YOU GET IF YOU CROSS THE INCREDIBLE HUNK WITH A RABBIT?

WE DON'T KNOW—TO CROSS THE HUNK YOU'D HAVE TO BE CRAZY!

GRR!

WHY DOESN'T THE HUNK KEEP HIS GOLDFISH IN A TANK?

THE ARMY ASKED HIM TO PUT THE TANK BACK WHERE HE GOT IT!

WHY DID THE TODDLER BITE THE INCREDIBLE HUNK?

MUM TOLD ME TO EAT MORE GREENS!

WHAT HAPPENED WHEN THE INCREDIBLE HUNK TRIED KARAOKE?

HE WAS A ROARING SUCCESS!

WHY DO THE POLICE KEEP CHASING INCREDIBLE HUNK?

NEWSAGENT

WE CAUGHT HIM SHOPLIFTING!

SIDEKICK WANTED!

CAPTAIN FABULOUS,
THE CITY'S NUMBER ONE SUPERHERO,
IS SEEKING AN ASSISTANT HERO

Must be willing to do all the dirty work, defy
death every day, give all credit to Captain
Fabulous and make the tea. No money is offered
but the lucky applicant gets to spend 24 hours
a day in the company of Captain Fabulous. Wow!

(PS. This is the 60th time this job has been advertised.
The Captain just can't understand why so many people
seem to be put off by having to make tea.)

WHAT'S A SUPERHERO WITHOUT HIS COSTUME?

(ER... ARRESTED, USUALLY).

BUT NEVER FEAR, THE JOKE BUSTERS ARE HERE WITH YOUR CUT-OUT-AND-KEEP

COSTUME!

IT'S ON THE NEXT PAGE AND IT'S FREE!

THERE YOU ARE, READERS — EVERYTHING YOU NEED TO MAKE THE COSTUME OF **PAPERBOY**, THAT AMAZING SUPERHERO WITH THE POWER TO FOLD, CREASE AND CRUMPLE UP INTO A BALL!

UNFORTUNATELY, THE ONLY THING HE **CAN'T** DO IS BE SEEN AGAINST THIS PAPER BACKGROUND!

42

Joke Busters
Guide to
REAL VILLAINS

NUMBER

3 DYNAMIC DOG!

What is its super power?
Able to hear very high-pitched sounds. (OK, we know every dog can do this.)

What is its secret identity?
Cute little puppy.

Where is its secret hideout?
Anywhere the postman doesn't expect him to be.

What is its weakness?
If the postman could find that out, we might actually get some letters now and then.

SUPERVILLAINS IN FOCUS!

Name: The Kitty Woman

Superpowers: Very sharp claws and even sharper costume.

How did you get your powers? I bought them, dahling ... I only shop in the best places.

Haven't you realized that crime doesn't pay? I don't pay either... That's why I'm banned from shopping in all the best places.

Aren't you scared of the police? Yes ... but only the fashion police.

Your motto: So much shopping to do, so little time. (And that includes all nine of my lives.)

THE SPY-MAN

JOKE FILE

THIS HERO REALLY IS IN A GLASS OF HIS OWN. A "SPYGLASS", THAT IS! AGENT GROAN

WHAT'S SPY-MAN'S FAVOURITE PLACE IN THE PLAYGROUND?

KEEP OFF

THE MAGNIFYING GRASS.

WHAT'S SPY-MAN'S FAVOURITE TYPE OF TV SHOW?

"FLY ON THE WALL" DOCUMENTARIES.

49

Joke Busters
SUPERHERO SECRETS

FLEX THOSE MUSCLES!!

MIGHTY MAN
REVEALS THE SECRET OF
TEARING A PHONEBOOK IN HALF! →

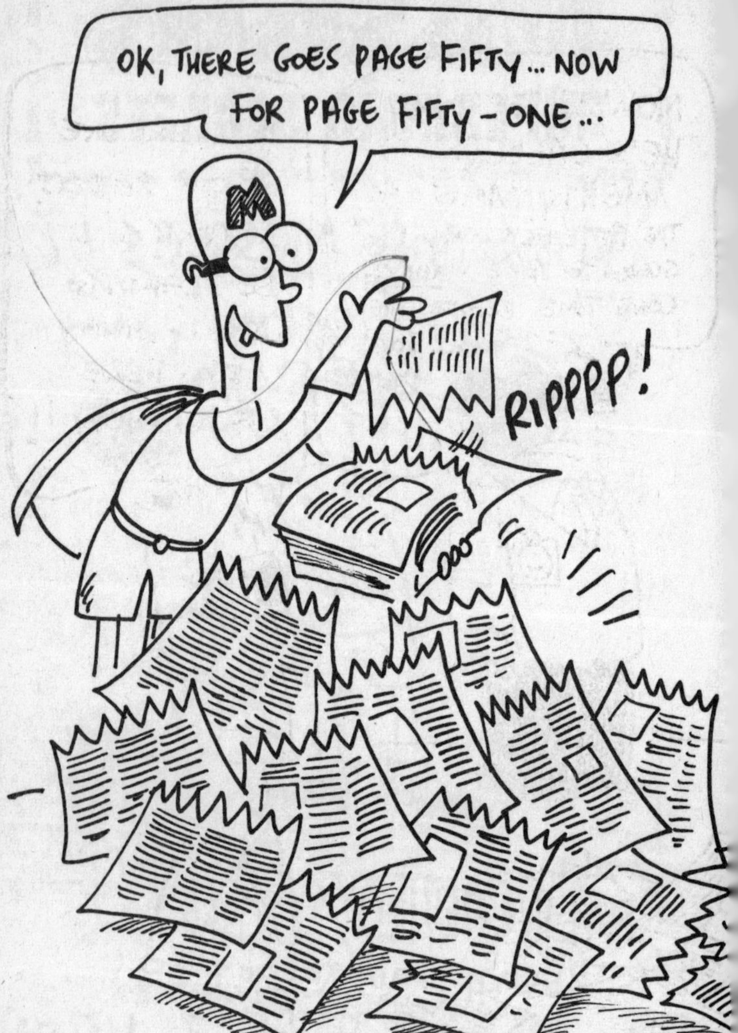
OK, THERE GOES PAGE FIFTY... NOW FOR PAGE FIFTY-ONE...
RIPPPP!

53

55

THE HEROIC HERALD

HAVE THIS NEWSPAPER DELIVERED FASTER THAN A SPEEDING BULLET!

(SEE INSIDE!)

HOP IT, WANDA WOMAN!

Rumours that Wanda Woman is *not* a superhero but is in fact a fairy godmother in disguise were given further impact today when she turned her latest opponent into a frog. Unfortunately her latest opponent was a 30-foot dinosaur which was trashing the city, and frankly a 30-foot frog doesn't do much less damage. Wanda Woman then warned this reporter not to cover the story or else, but I refuse to be silenced by... ZAP! Er ... ribit, ribit, ribit.

61

THE Z-MEN JOKE FILE

This is a whole team of superheroes with unusual powers they have to keep hidden from humanity. These jokes will show you why! AGENT GROAN.

DO THE Z-MEN TAKE ON IMPOSSIBLE MISSIONS?

NO...JUST ONES THAT ARE EASIER ZED THAN DONE!

WINDY WOMAN

Why DID THE Z-MEN DIVIDE THEIR HIDEOUT INTO FOUR!

BECAUSE ITS OUR HEAD-QUARTERS!

CHAIN SAW

63

Joke Buster's
Guide to
REAL VILLAINS

NUMBER **4** **POWER, PIMPLE!**

What is its super power?
Resists spot creams, pimple powder, anti-acne applications and even – YUCK – squeezing!

What is its secret identity?
Well, you could colour it with shoe polish and pretend it's a beauty spot.

Where is its secret hideout?
Hideout? Huh! It's blindingly obvious to everyone whenever you've got somewhere important to go!

Name: The Green Gobbler

Why do you eat so much? I'll tell you later ... don't want to speak with my mouth full.

Are you interested in taking over the world? No. But I'm interested in all the takeaways in the world.

Why are you green? Believe me, if you ate as much as I do, you'd be green too.

Who's your favourite superhero? Not sure. I haven't had a chance to taste them all yet.

KNOCK KNOCK!
WHO'S THERE?
SUPER!
SUPER WHO?
SUPER-ISE, SUPRISE... IT'S A BUNCH OF SUPERHERO KNOCK KNOCKS!
KNOCK KNOCK!
WHO'S THERE?
THUMP!
THUMP WHO?
THUMP-THING YOU'LL ONLY FIND OUT IF YOU OPEN THE DOOR!

THE JOKESTER

JOKE FILE

This Guy Dresses up like a clown— but if he catches you, it's no laughing matter! AGENT GROAN

WHY DID THE JOKESTER CROSS THE ROAD?

I HAD TO, YOU FOOL... THERE WERE SEVERAL SUPERHEROES CHASING ME!

HOW MANY SUPERHEROES DOES IT TAKE TO PUT IN A LIGHTBULB?

NONE! THE JOKESTER STOLE OUR LIGHTBULB!

WHAT'S THE DIFFERENCE BETWEEN THE JOKESTER AND A SCULPTURE MADE FROM OLD SOCKS?

WHIFF!

NIFF!

NOTHING - WE'RE BOTH NASTY PIECES OF WORK!

WHAT SHOULD YOU GIVE THE JOKESTER ON HIS BIRTHDAY?

A WIDE BERTH, SAME AS EVERY OTHER DAY!

HAPPY BIR-

HOW DID THE JOKESTER GET OUT OF PRISON IN THE FIRST PLACE?

I WAS PAST MY "CELL BY" DATE.

NUMBER 5 ROOM of DOOM!

What is its super power?
Resists cleaning and tidying no matter how many times you try.

What is its secret identity?
Sorry ... everyone knows it's your bedroom (and your job to tidy it!).

Where is its secret hideout?
Actually there's so much mess in there, you could have an entire army hidden in there for all we know.

SUPERHEROES IN FOCUS!

Name: Diredevil

Surely a superhero isn't scared all the time? Of course not ... only when I'm awake.

When's that? All night long ... I'm too scared to sleep.

So why don't you get into a different business? I would ... but I'm scared of change.

Your superhero hero: The Incredible Hunk.

Why? Because he said that he'd thump me if I didn't vote for him.

SECRET LAIR

FOR SALE!

Hi, it's the Jokester – arch-enemy of Batbloke and Robert.

Since the Dozy Duo haven't actually caught me yet, I need to move to a bigger place so I'm selling my secret lair, lock stock and barrel (full of dynamite, of course).

GREETINGS, DAHLINGS! IT IS I, THE KITTY
WOMAN, HERE. YOU SEE? WE SUPERVILLAINS
ARE UPFRONT ABOUT WHO WE ARE — BUT
AS FOR THOSE PESKY SUPERHEROES. HUH!
ALL THOSE MASKS AND CAPES AND HIDDEN
IDENTITIES. HOW DO THEY EXPECT ME TO
POP ROUND FOR TEA? (WELL, ACTUALLY T.N.T.)
NOT ANY MORE THOUGH. TURN THE PAGE FOR
THE ULTIMATE SUPERHERO SECRET:

THE IDENTITY OF EVERY HERO REVEALED!

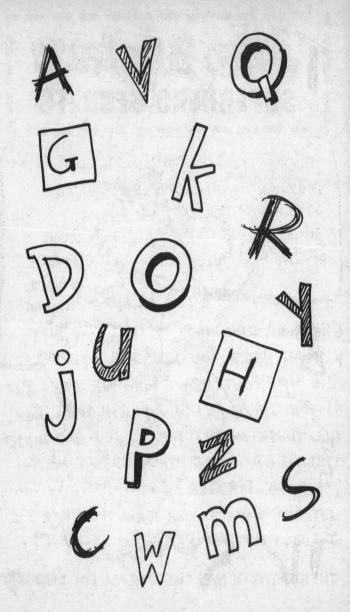

NUMBER 6 MIGHTY MOBILE!

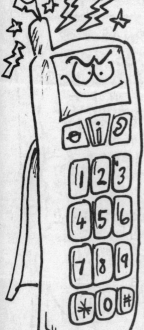

What is its super power?
None ... but you need to use hypnotic mind powers to persuade your parents to get you one.

What is its secret identity?
You think it's an easy, cheap way to keep in contact with your mates.

Where is its secret hideout?
You're going to need one when your parents find out how much money you've been spending on text messages.

SUPERHEROES IN FOCUS!

Name: Splash Gordon

You're an outer space hero? No. I work underwater.

Don't you get very wet? Hey, if at first you don't succeed, dry, dry again.

That's a terrible joke: Why do you think they threw me in the water?

Is there much crime to fight down there? Oh yes, we have a lot of famous criminals, like Billy the Squid.

Have you caught him yet? Yes ... but he had so many tentacles I ran out of handcuffs.

SUPERHERO A TO Z

A is for ADVENTURE !

WHY DID THE SUPERHERO WRITE A BOOK CALLED "MY WATCH IS SLOW"?

BECAUSE IT WAS HIS LATEST ADVENTURE!

B is for BATBLOKE !

WHAT IS BATBLOKE'S FAVOURITE GAME?

BAT-A-CAKE!

SUPERHERO A to Z

C is for CAPE!

WHAT DID THE CAPE SAY TO THE SUPERHERO?

I'VE GOT YOU COVERED!

D is for DIREDEVIL

WHAT'S DIREDEVILS IDEAL PET?

A SCAREDY CAT!

SUPERHERO A TO Z

E IS FOR ENERGY!

WHICH SUPERHERO HAS THE MOST ENERGY?

BATTERYMAN!

F IS FOR FEAR!

WHY DIDN'T THE SUPERHERO KNOW THE MEANING OF THE WORD "FEAR"?

A SUPER-VILLAIN HAD HIDDEN HIS DICTIONARY!

G IS FOR GREEN!

WHY WAS THE INCREDIBLE HUNK FIRED AS A TRAFFIC WARDEN?

STOP!

EVERYONE CROSSED WHEN THEY SAW THE GREEN MAN!

SUPERHERO A TO Z

H IS FOR HERO!

WHAT DOES THE CROWD SING AT SUPERHERO FOOTBALL MATCHES?

HERO WE GO, HERO WE GO, HERO WE GO!

I IS FOR INVISIBLE!

WHY DID THE INVISIBLE WOMAN THROW AWAY HER NEW COSTUME?

SHE COULDN'T SEE HERSELF WEARING IT!

J IS FOR THE JOKESTER!

K IS FOR KAPOW!

SUPERHERO A to Z

L IS FOR LASER VISION!

M IS FOR MASK!

SUPERHERO A TO Z

N IS FOR NUCLEAR! POWER!

WHAT DO RADIOACTIVE SUPERHEROES HAVE FOR LUNCH?

FISSION CHIPS!

O IS FOR OUCH!!

WHY DO SUPER HEROES CARRY BANANA SKINS?

SLIP!

TO MAKE CROOKS SLIP UP!

SUPERHERO A TO Z

P IS FOR THE PUN-GUIN!

WHO'S THE LAST PERSON THE PUN-GUIN WANTS TO MEET AT THE SOUTH POLE?

THE CHIEF OF POLE-ICE!

Q IS FOR Quack!

WHAT HAPPENED WHEN DUCKGIRL FOUGHT THE GIANT SPIDER?

I GOT WEBBED FEET!

SUPERHERO A TO Z

R IS FOR RESCUE!

HOW DID THE SUPERHERO RESCUE HIS GIRLFRIEND FROM THE RUNAWAY TRAIN!

HE BOUGHT A 'SAVER' TICKET!

S IS FOR SUPERHERO!

WHAT HAPPENS WHEN YOU GET BITTEN BY A CAN OF RADIOACTIVE BEEF BROTH?

SOUP

YOU BECOME A SOUPER HERO!

SUPERHERO A TO Z

T IS FOR TEST!

TO CHECK OUT THEIR CAPE-ABILITIES!

WHY DO SUPERHEROES HAVE FLYING TESTS?

U IS FOR UNDERPANTS!

WHICH SUPERHERO KEEPS FORGETTING HIS UNDERPANTS?

FLASH GORDON!

DON'T LOOK!!

V IS FOR VILLAIN!

HOW DO WE KNOW THE JOKESTER IS ABSENT-MINDED?

HE LOSES ALL HIS BATTLES!

GRR!

SUPERHERO A TO Z

W IS FOR WANDA WOMAN!

X IS FOR X-RAY VISION

SUPERHERO A TO Z

Y IS FOR **YELL!**

WHY DO KUNG-FU SUPERHEROES SHOUT SO LOUD?

...BECAUSE THEY HAVE HA-IIIIIIII PITCHED VOICES!!

Z IS FOR THE **Z-MEN** !

IS IT EASY TO JOIN THE Z-MEN?

NO, BUT I USED MY CLAWS TO CUT THROUGH THE RED TAPE!